LIFE, DEATH, LOVE, & BABIES

poems & writings by

DAVID BREHMER

Finishing Line Press
Georgetown, Kentucky

LIFE, DEATH, LOVE, & BABIES

Copyright © 2023 by David Brehmer
ISBN 979-8-88838-067-3 First Edition
All rights reserved under International and Pan-American Copyright Conventions. No part of this book may be reproduced in any manner whatsoever without written permission from the publisher, except in the case of brief quotations embodied in critical articles and reviews.

Publisher: Leah Huete de Maines
Editor: Christen Kincaid
Cover Art: "Skeleton" painting by Jeannine Chappell
Author Photo: Nissa Brehmer
Cover Design: David Brehmer

Order online: www.finishinglinepress.com
also available on amazon.com

Author inquiries and mail orders:
Finishing Line Press
P. O. Box 1626
Georgetown, Kentucky 40324
U. S. A.

Table of Contents

Motorcycle 1
Hakomi Walk 3
Routine 5
The Zen of Surviving 6
A Silly Little Lament 7
A Quiet Moment 8
Renewables 9
For Jack 10
Inheritance 12
So, So 13
There Are People 14
What I Mean When I Say the Words:
    An Introvert Attempts Explanation 15
Food of Love 17
Visiting Home in September 18
Elegy for a Monday 19
You Know? 20
Metaphor Test 21
Another Time It Might 23
Your Third Eye 26
The Constant Water 27
Upon Seeing Alex 28
Red Glare 30
Taking a Shower 31
Wow 32
Bath Hair 34
The Bargain 36
Anniversary 38
Tender Age 40
Raffi Said There'd Be Days Like This 41
Modern Love 42
We Return to Dirt 44

A Lonely Visit 46
A Certain Type of Light 47
Lightning Books 49
The Right Words in the Right Order 50
It's Art 51
Halloween 52
The Camp Fire from a Distance 54
For Daniel Ari on the Occasion of His Birthday 55
Where, Then, Are We to Go? 56
Home 57
Work Haiku 58
Clay Street and Jones 59
The Mundanity of Sex 61
On Heroes 63
A Dramatic Monologue to be Performed Without Audience 64
Waiting Behind a Stalled Car on the Highway 66
And Still Today 67
"Essential" Work 68
Status Report 69
The Novelty of Theft 70
500,000 72
To 39, Then 40 73
We and the Wildflowers 75
Time (Life, Death, Love, and Babies) 78

ACKNOWLEDGEMENTS 80

ABOUT THE AUTHOR 81

For Nissa, who believes our dumb world needs all the art, and Jack, who dances because he can't help it.

I love you.

Motorcycle

Spiderwebs arrived quickly,
stitching the weathered canvas cover
to his motorcycle tire.

The machine leans in the center of the yard, waiting
at the head of gradually disappearing ruts.
The tall grass weaves among the spokes,
weeds ground into graying treads.

The grass edges a wide dirt patch,
the shadow of his trailer, recently removed.

His belongings sit in a makeshift enclosure;
the tarp sags, revealing its pipe framework.
Sunlight slips in at bare corners like a pin
between the thumb and nail.

Water drips on milk crates and boxes.
The swollen wood of his dresser drawers cradles
dust-powdered circuit boards,
jars of orphaned ball bearings.

Assembled on the gravel is a small history,
an archive, begun and ended.

I walk among it expecting it to breathe.
It sits.
Resting, ready.

Unfamiliar odds and ends turn memories,
insightful and expected. So like him.
So like the time we.
So like I imagined he was.

"It's junk you know." I tell myself.
"He's dead you know." I answer.

Spiderwebs arrive quickly.
Even in a day they stitch together
objects at rest.

Hakomi Walk

He is at fault, of course,
but he does not become fault—
a skinless, rootless mass.

He walks and warms the bones
of other, luckier souls.

The heart hardens, constricts,
and stumbles to insist he is nothing
but a mistake.

Lost.

I remember the face of the one he doomed.
The patient eyes and the wet, horrible noise.

The piercing fire in my gut and knees.
The dawning I was not the one who died.

Alone.

In bed I tried to rid him of his life,
remove his weight and clear him
from our soil,

but his steps are burdened
and his bones are cold.

Open.

He is mine and I am his and we share roots
in drought and flood.

we know eyes and long to rid
ourselves of noises in our skin.

We walk and warm the bones
of those without.

Unclosed.

Routine

Along the shadowed, pre-dawn highway, wedging
into the swiftly glutting lane over and inching by
the rider's silhouette, rimmed in intermittent orange.
The hazy glow of tow truck headlights catches wrinkles
of a leather jacket, reveals a helmet laying upright,
empty on the pavement.

And passed and all arriving now at once, rushing brain
and clenching gut, electric limbs and fingers tapping,
triggered switch and flooding, tears and humming scar
and yawning absence looming also always racing close behind,
beyond the edge of vision and below the mirror's edge, striking
quick and violent, reverberating harsh and resonant through blood
and fear and cold, relentless silence, masks and steady burning
nights and should haves, will nots, forceful new realities, through
tender, tearing shreds of such alarming, potent humanity
and tedious waiting and waiting to return to some part
of what was and always knowing it is not and knowing
there is likely no end. No end but his. No end
but whose might come. One night. One morning. One call.
One turn. One fresh, relentless understanding.

And the rider lies alone. A family sleeping,
waiting, unaware that life is now a new beginning.
Time will now slink forward from what was.

The Zen of Surviving

Trauma lodges
in one's joints
like shrapnel,

sometimes burning,
sometimes tearing,
sometimes waiting
to burn.

A Silly Little Lament

Oh brain, you idiot,
don't you know you're me?

A Quiet Moment

—for Jeannine Chappell

There is no necessary clean and wooden gloss room floor,
cross-legged and quiet, incense carving upward,
tumble blue and thickly fading,
pouring faintly undulating grace
among the hushed and easy swell of simulated strings.
No white linen chakras, beckoned
open by ragged guru mats required
to pay honor to the graceful pains of ancients.
Neither tapestries nor cotton flags
nor comely Eastern trinkets prime the soul
for closer complements to sweetly severe ascetics
or casually needy Buddhas.

Just a spot to sit, straight-backed and supple,
open mind and courage flexed to meet
what then may enter.

But let alone that itch.
Leave it perch and nibbling.
Feel the crackle spread and ebb,
knowing fear is all that holds us stunted.

Renewables

One rarely imagines the end of trees.
We fret sometimes about fewer trees elsewhere,
but our boulevards remain more or less intact
in perfect spring gentle clapping breeze and color
memories.

One does not let creep a desert overlay outside
one's door. There may be fewer lawns, but parks
maintain their kept expanse and opportunity.
Grass is still vibrant after the rain.

When the perfect crab apple blossom hulk takes ill;
when the storm decides its needs outweigh the maple's;
one notices how unyielding summer sun has always burned.
One notes how faded grass has turned outside the shade
perimeter.

One does not imagine the end of children.
We fret sometimes about fewer elsewhere,
but our schools remain more or less intact
in inevitable spring hall squeak and t-shirt
always.

One does not let creep a plague wipe clean.
There may be tragedies, but parks remain
an endless hive of germs and adventure.
Eyes still shine with fear and abandon.

When one's own hallway suddenly falls silent;
when the playground looms a screaming web of ghosts;
one understands how heavy a dull eye can be.
One remembers this has happened and will happen again.

For Jack

We haven't met,
but I'd like to welcome you.
There are a few things to know
before you start.

On occasion, we will be upset.
This is not your fault.
It is a natural reaction
to fear and disappointment.

Fear is something you will learn about quickly.
Disappointment will take a while.
Neither is very fun.

Fun is a unique sensation,
tempting to chase, but most honestly experienced
through genuine connection to one's self,
one's surroundings, and one's companions.

Your first few years here will be relatively intense.
You won't explicitly remember much,
but will begin to absorb and develop
what defines humanity.

Humanity is a tricky thing.
It can be triumphantly exhilarating,
sensuously common, and bleakly disappointing.
But, again, that will come later.

Dirt is terribly important
for many reasons, not least of which
that it is fun (see above).
Politely ignore any who disagree.

You are entering a complex system
of conflicting ideals, competing interests,
difficult choices, strange outcomes,
and unexpected circumstances.

We are here to keep you alive,
to help you when needed when we are able,
and to remain a reliable anchor
in your rapidly expanding universe.

Get dirty, have fun, know fear
so you can learn to understand and ignore it.
Have patience, but do not hesitate
on your journey to becoming human.

Welcome. I cannot wait to meet you.

Inheritance

>—for my parents

The system seems perfect,
laid out in observable steps,
each comprised of complementary formations,
actions and reactions, necessary specificities,
all on schedule.

Life evolves, begetting life,
supporting evolution,
the instinct to continue, to protect, to enrich.

The pattern lives and builds,
informed by each succeeding incarnation,
patiently whittled towards the ideal,
absorbing eons of knowledge and nature,
alert to circumstance and need.

As I have learned and you were taught,
so will he be gifted the sum of all creation
until the very moment of his birth
and each day following. Our progress
his inheritance and charge.

The honor is mine to hand to him
the notebook and the pen, the toolbox
and the carving knife, the beaker and the voice.
I proudly offer all I have,
first given me by you.

The system seems perfect,
our hands evolved to carry, shape,
and pass along.

So, So

Toddling eyes
and wondering fingers,
back and toes and belly and skin
like paper, soft and so, so
almost impossible.
Breathing and kicking
and living now and seeing finally
and all and nothing before
and everything is suddenly everything,
blurring into something he won't remember
but will always know.
The sky and ceiling equal, endless,
speechless world of sound and light,
joyous, terrible, and awesome.
Home and family absorbed
and always now the one thing warm
and blessed common.
Hands wrapping minuscule and so, so
almost impossible.

There Are People

There are people in your life you assume will pick you
up from the airport, not because they are never busy,
but because, more often than not, they make it a priority
to be available for you.

They may do this for a number of reasons, kindness
and decency chief among them, but mostly it is because they assume
you would, at a moment's notice, drive to the airport
at 3 am to make sure they get home safely.

And you would, because they would, because family can mean
many things and still mean as much.

What I Mean When I Say the Words: An Introvert Attempts Explanation

I love you like
I love sunsets, suddenly spreading
out across life's tedium to radiate
the magnificent fact that the sun sets every day.

I love you like I love
the rhythm deathless in my bones,
waking my hips to slide subconscious
through the honey air
before I think to ask.

I love you like I love words
typed black with purpose and set
against blank and brilliant white
to mix the world and all its horrors.

I love you like I love the stupid gift of life.

I don't want to share a mortgage,
I want to dance with you like refugees
to the anthem of our invented homeland,
ecstatic to finally find another.

I want to spin and shuffle and beam until the sky
reminds us music must sometimes return
to dwell beneath our skin and hum,
bubbling inside until we are given again
the space to release.

I want you and your soul
to sit across from me and stare, to grin,
to glisten eyes and breathe the same rich air.

I want to create new life and breathe into it
all we know and hope. I want to carry
our creations to the shore, to scatter

them to the wind, to set them loose
in the forest and wait and watch until
it is absolutely certain they require
a friendly beacon.

I want to love you like a sponge accepts
water and we to be the hand that dips
the sponge and the glass that offers the liquid.
I want us to be the ripples and the lake and the rock
sinking swiftly to the mud,

and there, nestled beside the worms and fish scales
and fowl droppings, shine in the filtered light
an invitation to discovery for any who dare to swim
with eyes open, for those who know escaping air
and still choose to weigh new knowledge against time.

I love you like the fish we both eat and marvel at;
like the brick we stack like walls;
like the alarmingly smooth skin of a child, warm
like heaven; like the reassuringly worn touch
of a partner, like electric into yours in the blue
exploration of evening abandon.

I love you like I love.

Love like breathing roses and cheese.
Love like 2 am and burning for 3.

Yes, bills and time and terror and the insane, flailing remainder.
Yes, tomorrow and the next day.
Yes, our stupid, fading, miracle bodies
and our gorgeous, ambivalent planet.

When we can we will dance
beneath our ever-changing flag, ecstatic,
loving each other and wanting
to love.

Pushing our hips, whatever they may be,
against the pink and honey air.

Food of Love

> *"...play on..."*
> —Duke Orsino in *Twelfth Night*

The head waves quick in the space between two strokes
and all is steady, right, and pulsing, pushing, caving in and rolling
free and bound by time and expectation…

…no, by reassurance, welcomed, warm, embraced, and idolized;
thrust up and marveled from below, ripped down and frenzied
to amber moments, flashed and searing, building catalogs
of reflex bliss.

On the edge of resolution hangs the throat catch gut blossom
shouting beam of pinpoint focus, sweeping light, hands raised and
plunging deep into the split second sliver between synapse spark and soul,

snap, slide, and shudder, Goddamn holy, pure, and highest
new communion dripping salt and honey, whiskey, butter
and ambrosia spice lick acid, Kool-Aid, lemonade and gasoline.

Rumble grade school crush and hoping, veins pound ears,
anticipating touch, fresh and instinct flush, foundation, urging
forward, pop and hum, heart syncing with the rush,

lean back and cradled, riding, carried, pluck and thump, buzz,
thud, floor bounce through soles and up. The chest. The heart.
The gut. The bones. The spine and center merge, compress
and blow to pieces, oscillate, a speck in space, anchored
and without bounds.

Soaring, tilting, edging, tracing, carved and offered, pleading,
arching, kneeling, prodding, peeling, stripping, laying bare
and grooving, searching, mapping, stepping, closing eyes,
inhaling, melting, nursing, bleeding, crafted, building, honed,
believing

elemental ratios, transcendent and mundane, stitch together,
weld together passions, failures, grief, and progress,
tuned to spark a recognition born of instinct, bred by life.

Visiting Home in September

I take photos of the trees,
trying to bring the colors back with me,
hoping to conjure autumn at will.

I want the air.
Soothesingeing exhale crisp
and clear.
Damp and cooling leaves
and gutter crunch.

I want that medium jacket chill.
Wind and ear rim fingertips.
Early evening puff wisp breath
and pockets sleeve-tucked football
brownorange, yellowred, and green
resting there 'til winter.

I want to amble, gallery-paced
through leaf pile, playground, locker
combination, love, and roller hockey,
cider, campus afternoon bricks,
and maple outline windshield, pumpkin,
hay bale, pause

and marvel quiet, exhilarating bounty.
Sidewalk balance strings and now
the cymbal wash and sweeping redorangeyellow
green root-strong bluffs and swell,
eyes and chest and helicopter pan,
spiral down to seed-scattered pavement,
propeller stains and early evenings,
leaf stems piling in the seams.

But there is no magic in my art.
I am a buyer of woolen socks.
Autumn's purpose is to end.

Elegy for a Monday

Those M&Ms were a mistake,
just as I knew they would and will be,
but Ravel's "Bolero" retains its power
and gravitational nostalgia.

Such is life and magic
in this warehouse in San Jose.
Colder than one might expect,
yet not at all surprising.

You Know?

You know when you're sitting on the toilet at work
and you're staring at the floor
and the linoleum starts to swirl and shimmer
like heat rising off the asphalt in the middle of summer
as your car crests a hill and you look down into the valley
and the road melts into shallow, steaming pools
that catch the sun like the necklace of your elementary school
crush, blinding you for a fraction of a second
before the red-rimmed world returns, gradually fading into full
saturation, and the thought of the heat hits you like a cartoon,
panting and dragging himself in rags across the unforgiving sand,
sweat mingling with his three-day beard, lips cracked,
throat constricted with thirst, eyes widening as his hand weakly
stretches out towards the wavering paradise suddenly materialized
before him, replete with palms and fountains
and cocktail waitresses with silver trays and winking lashes,
and then you look out the sliding deck door to see it's gorgeous out
and you turn off the TV and grab your baseball glove and go next
door to see if our friend is busy, but he is, so you go back
to your yard and collapse, spread-eagled on the grass,
staring up at the impossible blue sky and listening to the birds
and the breeze and the giggling echoes of the kids at the pool down
the hill from the elementary school, and pause to think one day
you'll have to be at work in the summer on days like this,
but now you're just here right now with the breeze and the grass
poking through your t-shirt to gently prick your back?

Metaphor Test

"At sea" is apt, but insufficient.
The immediate vastness, the striking insignificance,
the unfathomable perimeter,
the muted, rolling calm

all evoke approximately the listless isolation, the myopic fear
of an anchorless void.
(But for the arrhythmic slapping of water against the hull,
the slow peace of a world so impossibly large.)

The sense of disconnection tracks,
the inability to signal, to step off quickly to land. (Though yes,
there are some who set themselves to sea for sport,
and some for employment.)

And it's true one may retire below deck, insulated
in bobbing familiarity when the clouds turn steel,
or remain above to face the graying distance,
open to more cutting winds.

What's missed is the actual proximity to shore,
the shallow depth of illusory contrast. Those on land
are heard clearly.
(They walk with purpose, carrying umbrellas.)

The calm is more a canceling out,
conflicting possibilities and parallels colliding quick
and humming cold.
(Fuses can be replaced. I know, I know.)

One has not been abandoned. There are no restraints.
One is free to walk off and join the others but does not.
(They are curious, but ultimately unconcerned
with your choice.)

You float alone in your sturdy, furnished world, aware
of the distance and depth, pacing
the deck as children wade in up to their shoulders,
tossing your ship unpredictably in their wake.

Another Time It Might

It might be her someday.
You might be the one bedside
waiting hard for that brief glint
of like before, smiling
to show you know
worse is possible
and luck is palpable, but
just like hell tearing inside
rip the walls scream fire
and tribute switch and
justice and FUCK.

You will have to remain calm.
You will have to see the tubes
and wires and bedsheets and remember
the feeling, the loneliness
and the monotonous inability.
You are the one now to speak
and note and negotiate
and dig and beg for information and courtesy
and remember when they don't
and remind them this is not
our job. Please just treat her
with some sense of sensitivity.
This is not her fault. Please
explain it and answer those questions
I do not know to ask.

The ceaseless intermittent beep.
The rushing wheels off kilter
in the hallway. The air of fresh
and stinging cleanser.
The needles. The tape.
The warm, plastic urinal. The stiff
and faded curtains. This
thick, closing aura of nothing you
want or want to be again

that hangs on every word
and pitying gaze.
Her skin still so soft. Her eyes.

You must look into her eyes
and declare the truth:
you are here bedside waiting.
You will be here with towels
and bedpans and ask her to
sip just a little more broth.
You will keep her away
from paperwork and signatures
and dollar amounts. You will
be there calm and ready
despite the grinding panic,
despite the lurking breakdown
horror, despite the racing
flashback specter solid behind
your eyes. You will be there
and know she needs you to be.

You needed her
and she sat waiting, running
straining, crying, pushing,
asking, forcing, feeding,
figuring out and never thinking
not to. There are truths
greater than what has been done
to you, to anyone, than what
has been taken or dismantled.
There are truths stronger
than nightmares and visions
and never agains soaking
through the pillowcase
in the still gray space before
dawn. There are jagged,
twisting truths that scream
the ineptitude of creation
and the glory

of barefaced humanity.
No matter what there is you
and her and your choice
at every step.

Your Third Eye

—for Nissa

The view through your third eye
is not reality, but truth,

life enhanced and crystallized
in ideal frozen moments.

Your vision holds, reveals,
our world as we know it to be,

not the way we see it,
but the way it breathes in our minds,

turning time into history
and connection into light.

The Constant Water

The resonant frequency of the bay is velvet,
a steady rolling bolt smoothed steady toward the rocks
by an invisible moon. Like breathing.

Duck back ripples intersect in perfect ratio,
harmonizing cross-pattern textures catching sun
and shadow blue-brown reflect rise and carry soft
to shore and out to fade into the coming wave.

One cannot penetrate the water,
eyes pulled gently back to the inevitability of the land,
feet in shoes on sand and gravel.

One remembers the shock fade chill of dangling ankles.
One remembers rising to turn and walk home.

Upon Seeing Alex

You were standing at the bottom
of the footbridge steps
as I passed, hand in hand, with my son.

I affected a swagger
and thought to myself,
"This is one thing I'll always have over you."

You paused, stone-faced,
and then erupted in a signature
bout of resonant elation,

just as I remember you
striding down Telegraph, barking
at my particularly dark Nazi joke.

The pavement stood starkly white
against the aimless blue sky,
the light casually harsh and uniquely Californian.

In your boots,
permeated with dust,
black, sleeveless tee and multi tool,

your heels struck the concrete
like a muted woodblock.
I don't remember what I wore.

We grinned to the car
with our remaining flyers,
both aware very few would show up.

And there at the bridge,
you grinned like before.
My son tripped and skidded to the curb.

You chuckled and shouted,
"Your son is a drunk."
Then jogged across the street to help.

Leaning over, you froze.
Eyes, still locked in honest concern,
fading to gray.

My son sucked his breath
and I turned to help him,
just the two of us under the aimless blue sky.

Red Glare

The plastic elephant shines frozen stars.
A planet, a moon glow red.
A tin chime cycle of Brahms's "Lullaby."
Our son's finger zealously skyward.

"Mooon!" he squeaks over and over,
torso and knees erratic.
Happy beyond smiling, he discovers the cosmos
five times in fifteen seconds.

And I strain to hear the arcing whistle
I know will not arrive.
Our private stars will likely not collapse
in rubble and ash.

The plastic elephant shines calm and red.
The darkness, his hand burn wonder.
I ponder how happy I have right to be,
how guilty and how grateful.

Taking a Shower

The twin-tone hum of the bathroom fan
sounds faintly of my son's plaintive cry,

just as the highway's constant roar
rings of chaos.

Wow

He bends to lift a rock from the sand,
his blind fingers probing the intricate caverns worn
by eons of salt and sediment.

The sunset painted chambers of the Apostle Islands
mold to his palm, washing patient
in glass bottom wake.

An iguana curls
its knowing toes around the stone's gentle angles,
flicking its gaze from the green-blue bay
to scuttling trails of porcelain shore.

Right under his chin,
a sheer face rises immortal, cresting treeline
sunlight magnitude and clouds shading valley pines
assured in Bridalveil mist.

His treasure shakes loose
black garden bed and trowel clink, embedded endless
petrified remains of glacial travel ancient lakeside reverent
toothbrush, dental pick and honored in between
Pez heads and alarm clock.

> Perhaps not eons, but months. How long does it take
> to carve, to shape? The smoothly safe shards of tumbled
> glass beside him resemble nothing
> so much as Heineken bones.

> The mussel shells at our feet look just like one
> I dropped in a clean, white bowl at dinner.
> Purple black and flecked with parsley.

He looks up to me, forgetting for a moment the nemesis
ocean foam swelling and receding to static behind him,
unaware of Bayfield, Wisconsin or Mexico,
or the monuments of California.

Unaware
of the Minnesota yard behind the house my family no longer
calls its own, he stands with his back to the infinite expanse,
offers his find, and blooms,
"Waaaow!"

Bath Hair

When my son's hair is wet
it looks like Walter Donovan's
in *Indiana Jones and the Last Crusade*
after he picked the wrong grail.

I mean to say his head resembles that of a fictitious,
decomposing Nazi.
Long, clumped strands hover across odd
empty patches. Tangled and thickthinbald.

His ultrasound was like some kind of H.R. Giger installation.
Pre-formed limbs and earfingers cresting from a swirling
grayscale miasma. His perfect turtle face bubbling up then sinking
back into the thickalgae protoplasm pond,
its crystal innocence branding the chaotic ether
all the more bizarre.

All this scored by the rhythm of his unflinching heart,
echoing heavy off of wood-grain laminate cabinets and tables,
riding cradled like a bobber in the tin ocean roar
of his mother's womb.

There is little if anything more beautiful
than understanding these surreally unique moments
to be the closest to pristine my life will likely get.

A woman once dove to cover her child's body
as a drunk driver t-boned their sedan.
The child's legs were severed at the hip, ankles contorted
behind his ears, eyes bulged in silent horror.

His mother leapt to spare him the sight of seeing her
silent beside him before his own last breath escaped.

Through her mind before she died rushed a random
series of silent wonders.
Her son's plaintive grimace when pooping.

The unadulterated heartbreak of his laughter.
His welcome tears when he chose her to wipe them away.

The Bargain

I met a woman who lost her son.
Her son had been my friend.
We bonded our grief together,
knowing it was not the same.

Separate, but parallel,
we push, not knowing where.
Simply forward, hard and through
as forceful as we dare.

My son was born and now I know
something of what she lost,
swaying in the back seat
singing that he knows the names of cars.

She loves my son in near the same
way that she loves her own.
She knows what we accepted
on the day we brought him home.

"I can't imagine." They all say.
She says, "I think you can."
The floor beneath your feet
is not as sturdy as it seems.

She knows what one phone call can do.
She knows how thin the tether.
She knows what color the box turns
as it rolls into the fire.

And she knows how fragile fingers are,
how warm tired shoulders.
She knows the wrenching pull through black
of love's undying smolder.

And I know too the risk involved,
the dam built just to breach.

What one allows inside
when one allows one's soul to reach.

The darkness guaranteed is all a part
of our grand bargain.
The day you feel those fingers curl,
your heart is broken
open.

Anniversary

It seems critical to mention it,
though much of me would rather not.
It's tempting to reframe it all
as something I've forgotten.
But framing begs precision,
begs measurement and foresight;
and efforts to adjust refine
my focus on that night.

One's memory should not be caged,
its tendrils flip and spark at will.
Through time and sentiment it roams
one's storage houses never filled.
On some it trips and sparks anew
senses recognized of old;
some are hunted, caked in dust,
damp in mounds of grief and mold;

others stacked and clearly labeled,
filed neatly for retention;
some are mounted separately
with honor and intention.
But some live crouched in shadows,
slipping coolly through the dark,
flashing unexpected
then returning to the murk.

Round these a persistent image clings,
ringing red the present day
with fear the remnant be replaced
at any time with the same
brief terror, quicker than a thought,
an agonizing second lost,
a message hung and left to rot,
a cruel reminder of the cost.

Invincible, these flashes stalk,
stinging with impunity.
At times provoked, at times alone,
regardless, one's whole self unpeels.
It's always fresh, although removed,
diluted from its mortal strength.
The fear becomes how strong
the next will be and how long it remains.

One fears the recollection,
not its formative event.
One rues the fact one's current state
was wrought without intent.
One yearns one's memory were tamed,
selective, if receding;
but to block the gasping end
would be to block the laugh preceding.

So one lives aware one's house is rigged,
conscious in the threat,
gut punch shock or doldrum mud
with each reminder met.
We walk unbowed by what has passed,
accepting all, and yet
we long for the impact's fade
while not trying to forget.

Tender Age

It wouldn't take much to break your finger.
A strong will and weak morals.
Like a twig if you would just stand still.

My son's three year old pinkie is thin like art class pottery.
His nails practically peel off when I clip them.
It would be easy to push too far.

I think of index pads hanging from fence wire diamonds.
The coiled confidence of a cage dweller, casual but ready,
stalking The Yard in Hollywood prisons.

I think of my son's pale mug handles pressed against the bars,
white impressions on reddening palms.
I think of his nails bent and peeling against metal.

I think how easy it would be to snap his digits,
but why?
He wouldn't know the reason.

He would know only my eyes and the sudden, outraged burn.
The muted crack would make clear
he had imagined the world incorrectly.

Raffi Said There'd Be Days Like This

You gotta stomp when the spirit grabs
you by the solar plexus and pulls
your essence to spin above the empty
bullet casings bouncing against
the cage fences steadily rising red
in the coming drought and flood.

You gotta stomp when the spirit
draws you to thank the clouds
you have legs to spread like power
to allow your air strum fist
phantom pound the patient Earth
to prove you live despite life.

You gotta stomp when the spirit
says stomp because there are some
who need you to remember existence
is worth existing, to turn
your lucky power towards those
the world has deemed do not deserve it.

Modern Love

I've probably heard "Modern Love"
a hundred times or so.
It's not a particularly good song,
but it's catchy and it's Bowie.

I remember hearing it when I was a child.
I remember remembering *My Fair Lady*.
I didn't know who Bowie was at the time.
I think I thought it might have been whoever sang
"Come On, Eileen."

Anyway, today it's on my Bowie playlist. R.I.P.
I had paused it halfway through to go to lunch
and just now put my earbud back in
after reading about the latest shooting in California.

It ended at a school. Some children were injured.
An elementary school. Again.
In the lingering shadow of the last
it probably won't garner much national attention.

We've seen this one before.
And it happens more than we've seen.
On corners in cars at concerts at home
in markets in rubble in custody.

I remember when I was a kid in the backseat
trying to figure out why on Earth this pop song
was written about Eliza Doolittle's father.
We had rented the VHS from the local library
and I was a big fan of accents.

I once caused quite a scandal when I neglected
to inform my parents I was going out with my friends
after we got together to study. And again when my band
covered some songs with vulgar language.

There's an undeniable comfort in choosing to hear a song
you've heard before.
It's an anchor. A blanket.
A place in which to rest.
Not like a sidewalk or a hospital bed,

more like a cave, huddled and quiet.
Away from what's happening now.

We Return to Dirt

A tree,
plains shadow hill

shortly rising sunset
seed tops whisper
and flies.

      Leaves respond
a harmony, percussive
in the still warm
breeze.

      The tree
notices how loud
the meadow lays
itself to sleep.

Within its fiber
it remembers back
home such silence
after returning from
the oscillating highway
wash of California,

his other home
in his other life.

The blanket sound
of next to nothing.

Flannel, bookshelf, glow-
in-the-dark solar system.

Those Minnesota nights
decades before without
sleep,

      fossilized
with unanswerable questions
at the desk,
pen or knife
in hand.

      Branches
now free from ever
needing to hold,

riding the breeze
like his palm
out the Highway 1
window that time
before what wound
up being true,

lying now atop
the wind without
ever needing to pull
back in.

      But where
did the seeds
of his family
scatter?

      Alone
at dusk, his
century-held roots
dig silent to
remember warmth.

He creaks softly
to maintain his
knowing.

A Lonely Visit

Dying, in all its strange translucence,
appears between two phases of existence
like a faintly yellowed film,
one through which we may reach
to touch those on the other side
and through which we must peer
to watch them go.

A Certain Type of Light

—for Liebe and Linda

There is a certain type of light
in a certain type of garden
where the sun does not bake
or pry or cover.

It lays atop each leaf,
patient to be received,
radiating the potential of each
green and hovering moment.

Hushed and buzzing green,
glowing bright and cool and ready.
Stirring, patient green,
glowing ageless and new.

But not ageless, ancient.
The fence post disappears inch by inch.
Shadows cut new angles
as the leaves grow dense with summer.

The sun arcs across the casually evolving landscape,
stretches and sinks each day closer
to pristine and rotting fruit.
Flies and blossoms buzz in turn,

bloom and wither and burn and be.
Beneath the sun the garden pulses,
hushed and standing, reaching imperceptibly
towards compost.

But to walk in that light, to taste
the peaches appear and swell,
to know the figs at each stage of their existence,
to smell the green and living world

caress and make way for and tower above
your silly, magnificent steps.
You smile and sit and join with her
and the Earth and everything.

The sun will find your upturned palm
and lay like her hand atop yours,
patient to be received.

Lightning Books

My four year old asked
what is electricity?
And, rifling high school notebooks,
still more margin doodles than information,
I searched my recollection
for a suitable point of entry.

After clear step footholds
of Grandma's house and August summer
and that steel gray sky we huddled
close under the posi-nega ion clouds,
we agreed that there was lightning
in the living room walls;

and I thought to myself, My God,
what magic it is to read in bed.

The Right Words in the Right Order

It's a street you know. The same street.
The same town and block and sky.
It's the same tree and the same eyes.

But today something turned you.
The pulse of the Earth summoned.
A subtle tilt, a whispered force.

You catch it at the mid-point of your stride,
rather than after your foot falls.
Just as your heel hovers above the concrete, the sun

permeates a single leaf, alone at the tip of a near-barren
branch. The veins burn red, floating
in a rippling pool of fiery translucence.

It waited for this fraction of a day.
It held its place, watching
the others quiver, snap, and feather to the grass.

Your heel crunches another, curled and brown,
and your steps carry you forward, away and on.
But the pool and the veins and the sun and the pulse

of the Earth remain yours.
Even if only until you reach for the doorknob,
for a moment the world was new.

It's Art

"It just doesn't do anything for me." She said.
He closed his eyes and nodded.
"Taste and quality are often at odds.
You need to know the context to understand
why this is good."
"Is this good?"
"It is."
"Huh. I guess I just don't understand art."

Nothing more is said.
One drifts, buoyed by a life preserver untied from its mooring.
The other sits on the dock watching the tail end of the rope
slip across the boards, appreciating the well-framed irony of it all,
admiring the metatextual sense of play.

"See, now this makes sense to me." She shouts
to the quickly receding pier.

Halloween

Tonight the veil is thin, they say.
Life walks nearby Death.
Souls and spirits sculpt new forms
from our old mortal clay.

Tonight we creep beneath the moon,
our costumes as our armor
against what might, but probably won't,
unified by our one truth:

we are all just grinning bones
wrapped in suits of meat,
clacking forward toward the one
that knocks our final trick or treat.

But be not sad that this be fate,
for it was ever thus.
Since shadows first stretched long on Earth,
we've known we have a date.

So stare Death in the eye and grin,
I know you know my name.
We are, beneath this pile of drying clay, the same
and there begin.

With moistened fingers we will work
ourselves to newer forms,
we'll high five Death and send our best
to those we miss left in the dark.

For though we wish reunion,
it's impossible to happen.
Revel that today you're here
with spirits as companions.

Don a sheet or scar or wig.
March into the night and
celebrate our gift of life
by laughing at what frightens.

The Camp Fire from a Distance

—November, 2018

Like the cool spark of evening stars,
the smoke that now defines our sky
has traveled many miles from its birth.

Across unfathomable distances,
the hearts of stars roil with cataclysms,
just as the flames that have birthed our inconvenience
burn far away a brilliant portrait of loss.

For Daniel Ari on the Occasion of His Birthday

You are one year less than fifty one
and fourteen more than thirty six.
The ocean rushes to chill your ankles,
then recedes.

Where, Then, Are We To Go?

We gather in groups,
the peace of disparate lives
connected by one elevated truth.
Be it faith, be it friendship,
be it music, be it love.
Like the calm of sleep
energized and expanded to surround
the waking world. To experience
the blank, individual comfort
and also see you are not alone.

We gather to meld with the confidence
of understanding we are tiny pieces
of an unknowable, yet no less awesome,
whole. Chaos muffled, priorities clear,
if only for the duration.

How cruel, then, to rip
into our most intimate shelters
with the vulgar cacophony
of a jealous and cowardly other.

How debased to be confronted
by petty hate at the heights
of our glorious potential.

How piercing the bullet
to the back of bended knees.

Home

There's a distinction to the bareness of Minnesota's winter trees.
They do not ring of death or loneliness.
They stand too vibrant to be still.

They breathe with the slow peace
of gestating spring.
They enunciate the inevitability of life.

Work Haiku

Apple blossoms skate
away from footsteps, ripples
on an asphalt pond.

Clay Street and Jones

It took 15 full minutes to park.
Finally, a car-length wedge of side street.
Parallel, downhill. Tires to curb. Feet to sidewalk.
Full force wind at 60 degree spine and trudge
past doorways and pee-stained planters,
over cigarette stubs and spiderweb cracks.
Echoed bleating slash from behind,
from out of the rush of the rest of them,
those not yet grounded at sidewalk pace.

And, cursing under breath at time and money
and dirt, you crest the hill and My God,
but out of absolutely nowhere the sun
breaks beyond a concrete corridor
and the ocean is just there down there casually
rolling back and forth as though
it wasn't sitting for a portrait of taking one's time.
The silent, penetrating awe of a Saturday
second down from the shadowed corner
to the absolute horizon.

Sky and asphalt. Water and tourists.
Beneath your feet, right there, right then,
the cables whir and click, pulling tram loads
up, away from this dumb miracle rimmed
by yachts and beverage carts, sparking
intermittent in the pulse of some large
ever-flowing hulk of joy and garbage.

Sparking skin caressing endless depths
of hidden wonders, pockets of fathomless
nothing, of unimaginable vibrance,
of unknowable provenance.
Below and beyond the sea.
Behind and between each concrete face.
Beneath our intermittent sparking skin
we flow from street corners like jelly

through the reef, floating blind until
we find ourselves in pieces on the shore,
suddenly alive in a wider world.

The Mundanity of Sex

It is the mundanity of sex that excites me,
streaked with mucus and semen,
panting with sweat and pulsing muscles
like a runner or a worker or a child.
All skin and meat stirred by an electric center
to push our name forward,
to merge and know our animal self is not alone.

We are mud and germs and horror.
We are dumb and beautiful apes who learned to talk
and trick each other.
We are stunning collections of potential amazement.

We have sex. We eat tacos.
We pick our noses
because it would be less comfortable not to.
We are fingernails and tongues.

Her palms against mine and vice versa,
locked in honest fervor, pressing into
with accepted confidence of place and possession
shared. Eyes and lips and fat and all
we have just then in the blue-gray universe.

She asked if sex was different after the baby,
but no of course not.
That's what it is,
what it does.
We do so many different rain-slicked, dingbat things.
We build and kill with the same hands.
We (she) create(s) life for the sole purpose
that it may be lived, entered into shaking and blank,
unfurling itself into endless corridors
of connection and possibility.
Her sex does not define, but expand her,
opening one more chamber of her endless potential.
A woman on fire. An animal. An artist. A mother. A technician.

A CEO padding her way over last century's leaves
to define necessity and want in the jungles
we assume eternal.

We are mucus and semen.
We are cowardice and genius.

We are The Four Seasons and we are hot dogs.

We are all of it compacted into our blue-gray universe,
sniffling and exploding into another day and night.
We merge to remind ourselves we exist, together,
animals searching for our place.

On Heroes

Perspective tricks and shifts
horizons stretching years
and lines point brainback shadows
into which one pair of eyes will see

and strain to cast back
unimpeachable, inescapable flesh
and graven stone.

But art,
but love and family and new fire
spreading worlds and histories.
Flash points and magic.
Influence.

And those eyes watching, underscoring,
cutting through and wrapping
idols, pulling, holding, flashing

windows, t-shirts, shot glasses,
and screens casting back
undisputed, inescapable
truth and everyone.

Everyone foregone casting
shadows behind them.

A Dramatic Monologue to be Performed without Audience

Lights up on an empty stage. FEAR enters wearing a black top hat and cloak. His lidless eyes are milky white and without pupils.
He stalks the stage with confident intensity and a pencil mustache. His gestures are large and dramatic.

>   FEAR
> Your affirmations are pointless. The world exists within and around you and does not care how you feel about it. This is the truth.
>
> Your insignificance is immense. Make no mistake.
> You are alone in your need to continue. No one will tell you when or what to do. This is the one,
> overarching certainty.
>
> Who are you to imagine your struggles meaningful in such a world as this?

FEAR turns his back and removes his cloak. When he turns again his eyes are green. His pupils wide in the light. The pencil mustache has grown out into a bushy red with matching beard. He stands center stage in his hat, a black button-down shirt and gray dress pants. His intensity is more restrained, but no less menacing. He stares straight ahead and speaks with a quiet, measured tone.

>   FEAR
> This is pointless, you know. I will not leave.
> I never do. I never have. I am a constant.
> I am the unifying feature.
> I am the unimpeachable truth.
>
> Why did you come to hear me speak if not
> to listen to what I say? Do not invite me in
> and then snivel for me to leave.
> Your pleas do not move me.
>
> I am life. Without me there is nothing.

FEAR unbuttons and removes his shirt. He unfastens his pants and drops them to the floor, kicking them to the side of the stage. Throughout all of this he does not once break his burning stare, but his rigid spine softens as the spotlight narrows. One beam shines pale in the darkness. FEAR stands quietly center stage in a black t-shirt tucked into blue jeans. He removes his hat to reveal an unkempt head of thick, auburn hair. His head bows slightly. His posture registers both shame and resolve.

                      FEAR
    Why do you do this? You know how this ends.
    We're going to stick around.
    You're going to stick around. Cycle. Repeat.

    I'll let you in on a secret. We don't care either.
    We're just here. We're always here.
    It's up to you to live next to us
    and not listen.

    It's always just you. Alone.

FEAR pulls a chair from out of the shadows and sits, soft eyes fixed straight ahead, as the lights fade to black.

Waiting Behind a Stalled Car on the Highway

Cold sweat knuckle pinch
and acid rising headlight growing
always never space enough
and nowhere else and now
and now and wait and what if never
who and how and sorry and stupid
and armpits now and spine and
toes curl to press and held and
held by what exactly what
and now no now no no now
NEVER no NO NOW NOW NOW NOW
mirror gas and throat and eyes and fingers
feet and knees and phantom impact arch
away and settle knowing now is not the time.

And Still Today

That insidious crunch behind the wall
rises from a whisper to a piercing
sort of silent tinnitus, gently scraping
at the edges of my skull,
tripping the projector looping sudden
pricks of marrow burn and memory,
a mask of flooding, sunlit terror.

A rush of plaid and taillights twisting
sharp and detail-perfect, stitches, dirt
and console divots, glasses, ankles,
floor, and pavement spark
and black
and afternoon clouds like elementary school
hallways and my son, born after the pain,
tripping in his blind elation
through the puddles he made himself.

The plaid and the puddles and regret
and drunken ego and sprouting life
and his mother who dreams in the past
and *his* mother who squints into the future
and the plastic egg halves from Easter
now boats, now balls, now forgotten
in the driveway and the joy
and the crushing, phantom gravity

and it's Tuesday now and it will likely be Wednesday
and I'm wanted with the spray bottle
and the food coloring
and how many years of life have led me here,
knowing I can't protect my family
from chaos.

And his immature hand on my shoulder
pulling me through the need
to remember it all.

"Essential" Work

72 mph for 45 miles straight,
riding curves like breathing,
like I have pined for nine years
of brake light mornings
and tail pipe afternoons cursing
the sheer amount of people traveling anywhere.
Now, finally able to measure distance
in minutes, I curse their absence,
curving towards blank inevitability
and home.

Status Report

Hope is a thing with feathers
and the clouds are dropping oil.
We're in waders clutching paper towel
and soap.

The weather folks predict a steady rain
from here on out
and the ones in charge suggest
we burn our coats.

The Novelty of Theft

Immediately upon entering the world,
our lungs know to draw in the atmosphere
of our new home. Never a thought,
rarely a question, the body, recognizing
need and newfound space, expands
to fill the nest prepared ahead of time.

Through every lesson of mind and muscles
after, we collapse into our constant pillow
of breath to remember we are nowhere else
but here and in this moment tasting life
without the need to try, focus painting
the potential of anatomy.

Sternum and diaphragm under shoulders,
capped and re-directed out in two smooth
sweeps like dancing. Command grace
to tempo and work to marshal
what we can control in panic,
pushing rhythm to subsume.

Imagine instinct batted away,
the grasping rush of falling further than expected
into less than is required, never comfort,
only just enough to not strike concrete.
Neck and laterals lift tense to drag a thread
of air to coat the limp and straining lungs,

tearing heavy to pull yourself back
to a body certain of support, idling
in the background, ready to be anchor
in the eye of all the world can stack
upon your open frame.

Now imagine severing the cord
of another carrying your need and organs,
fiber by fiber removing their ability to hold

against the weight of time. They recognize
the absence and will never again fill the home
they have prepared.

Exhale and imagine their right to breathe is not assured
as yours. How easily do you next draw in your share?

500,000

It would take a passenger jet
roughly 34 days
to travel 500,000 miles.

600 mph with no stops for gas.
Impossible.
It is an impossible amount.

Yet families learn quickly
every lofty tally is built
on single pairs of empty hands,

more possible than even math.

To 39, Then 40

I'm getting older like everyone else,
waxing heavy and reactive,
my chest resting acid and yearly rings
exposed to chart the countless warnings
offered in the face of my strange confidence
against physics. The early gifts of metabolism
project select immunities to entropy, until
a year of mirrors and medications force
a reckoning with shadows and time,
the slow work of maturity finishing
its bridge to the present to finally judge
the chasm between death is inevitable
and life is long if you're lucky enough
to live to fade beneath the stars.

Back wooden with sitting.
Knees trigger happy tender.
Belly rolling the waistband of my underwear.
Hairs sprouting absolutely everywhere.
Mind drifting between the past and a blank future,
grinding heavy to conquer the puzzle
through conjectured revisionism,
piling indictments and judgements with no
clear plan for rehabilitation, just a thick rope
of alternate endings tethering one ankle
to my decade-weary desk and scraping noticeably
across the scar-worn linoleum beneath me.

But a butterfly flaps its wings and we get rain
and you hurriedly duck into the Walgreens only to see Her
reading a magazine in a t-shirt that confirms your faith
in serendipity. And what if you had remembered your jacket?
What if you had spent more on your umbrella?
What if you ever bothered to look at the weather
before leaving the house? You, rumpled mess
of contradictions, are unique in the modern world
and kicking through a universe of special, ragged piles

each blown like blue Murano into pristine, purposeful icons.
And maybe no one needs a giant, opalescent
stallion, but there's a shelf just waiting all the same.

There are answers, some will say, and some will be right
and some will be easy and some will boil your muscles
to extend themselves through the nearest fucking drywall
and some will curl you up like some brittle-skin, gutter-blown leaf
and pin you to the felt with all the sympathy of an eighth grade
science lab. Maybe this is it for you. Maybe you
should get the fuck up. Maybe you should use those charts
like inverse maps and start walking. Maybe your heart
is the exact correct distance from your brain stem
and maybe you owe it to the stars to keep yourself polished
and ready for display.

My joints have withered behind imposed limits
and have embarrassed expert terminations.
I remember the wild fear of stepping out beyond
and the sick chill of recognizing myself incapable.
The brain ripples itself into corners it imagines cells
until a sudden breeze tickles its focus from the wall.
Severed cords are easily re-tied.
Trust in monsters manages the certain depth of myths.
There exist many paths corroded with vines
and my machete sharpens as it eats.

I'm getting older like everyone else,
waxing closer to full in a system
of indeterminate phases, breathing
under the potential of the stars.

We and the Wildflowers

The goddamned flowers are like magic,
dotting the coastal hills like dashes of self-contained fire
flickering in the mist of the unfathomable ocean,
perfect in their delicate thousands.

They burst through clay and cling to stone and spring
after months and years of dormancy into startling life
under a few rare drops of desert rain,
magic and buzzing spirituality.

But I've seen the diagrams. I've read the histories.
Root and pistil, seed and photosynthesis.
The birds, the wind carry these opportunities.
Sinew fingers dig for water. Specific colors

stir bees and bugs. All is in service
of staying alive and all is neatly observed and explained.
Still, the unnamed chemical combustion bursting within
our phantom, human hearts drips with wonder and deference
at the sight of science painted quiet.

We stand and walk and listen and watch
the news and cut our fingers on broken glasses
in the sink and stir ourselves with fear and money
and time and loss and yearning and wondering

how short have we fallen of whose goal and who
is going to do something about all these people?
We sit sometimes and allow the tide to wash us over.
We see through the water the cliffs above the shore,

dotted with sparks of patient life. We breathe
in water or air or smoke. We breathe the same air
that batters, caresses, ignores the flowers. We
inhale air expelled by those who do not understand
our air is leased.

Or do and don't care. Or do and don't know
what it is to share a set of initial conditions;
water and soil and air and light and time,
time to grow and learn and envelop oneself

in a world of one's choosing; setting and character
and plot and God. God who chooses which
wind and which train wreck. God who polishes
the linoleum unevenly and whispers in the ears
of those already late to wear socks and run.

God who poked a hole in a universe of nothing
and placed the seeds of existence and evolution
and consciousness and need.
We share this God, whatever it is.

Whichever world we choose is dotted in flowers.
Whichever God we choose, the conditions of our Earth
remain. Carbon and nitrogen babbling like idiots,
scrambling to carve some meaning out of the weird

lump of arbitrary clay before us. Hacking, coaxing,
urging, waiting for some coherent shape to appear,
cocked heads and wet fingers skimming the world as it spins,
millimeter by millimeter searching for the vessel to carry what may,

what might and Jesus, where did that guy learn to sculpt?!
How did she think of that and how lovely and terrible
is it that our own hands are all we have to translate ether
into matter? Sculpting side by side in buzzing rooms,
speckled with dots of airborne remnants,

the electrical flashes of our hearts and brains
wade through talent and experience and observation
to mold a vase for flowers.
Flowers plucked from hillsides and coasts,

from forests and deserts and swamps.
Flowers cut for shortened lives in buzzing rooms

and sunlit windows, sorted by color and size and smell
and meaning. Stuffed in school lockers, pinned to gowns,

strewn on bedsheets, dying in hospital fluorescence,
gathered in the thousands by cheap and starving fingers.
In the wild, we worship together at the flowers,
recoiling singed fingers from attempts to capture
their utilitarian flame.

We stand and walk and listen and watch.
We see through the water the cliffs above the shore.
We carry our vessels through the crowd,
returning to the wheel to share and hear our revelations,
humbled in our delicate thousands.

Time (Life, Death, Love, and Babies)

Oh, Time, you weird, relentless creep.
—David Brehmer

Walking with my son and dog, I often ponder
stray bullets. It used to be me, the one shocked and bleeding.
How would my son respond? Would he scream or run?
Would the dog lead him home or just stand there licking my face
and butting me with his anxious head?

Sometimes it was the dog. What kind of first aid instincts
would surface? What would my son retain
of the odds of his pets sprouting holes?

But now it is he, eyes wide with confusion and pain,
sweatshirt wet and legs unhinged against the concrete.
Would I freeze, obliterated? Would I think to call before
squeezing him to my chest? How much anger would
bubble how soon? If he lived, how would he...

My five year old son shrieks as a mourning dove
rustles into view in the tree up ahead.
He runs and trip hops forward, imitating it's owl song.
He bobs like birds-of-paradise, streaked with jungle shadows.

He loves to read our bird guide, incessantly requesting names,
pointing hard at strange crests and distinctive markings, watching
and re-watching *Planet Earth* in bottomless awe.
Africa is as far away as his wingspan and might
as well be Redwood Park.
Yesterday is last year and last year we saw a snail.

"Sometimes snails get squished." he recites a lesson
from years past, turning his head to double-check
our new friend's safety as we continue home.
"I don't like it when they are squished."
"Yeah, but it happens sometimes."
"Yeah." he admits softly, absorbing for next year, Friday.

He skids into the driveway and grabs his plastic bat,
motioning that I am to pitch to him a pinecone stand-in.
As he squares up to nothing, I stare a phantom catcher
into the neighbor's garage wall.

At dinner time, he pretends not to hear me and
I count to five before telling him again it is time
to go inside.

"But the sun is still out." he intones logically, with a tinge
of betrayal.
"True. But, it's dinner time." I counter good-naturedly.
"But, why?" he responds, still ready to swing.

I have no good answer. I pitch once more
and eventually coax him to stomp slouch in,
sobbing, "I want to be outside!" in a desperate
plea to his mother.

I have no good answer.

I will call my continually aging parents tomorrow
to tell them a funny thing he said yesterday.
Last year.
Thursday.

ACKNOWLEDGEMENTS

The author thanks Nissa Brehmer, Jack Brehmer, Steve and Linda Brehmer, Sarah Michna and the Michna family, the Brehmers, Findsens, Zellgerts, Schulls, Buttners, and Murphys, Jeannine and Sean Chappell, Liebe Wetzel, Linda Devers, Daniel Ari, Amos White, Gene Kahane, Jan Dederick, Anne F Walker, Marise Phillips, Kathleen McClung, Aditya Sharma, Kelly Williamson, Katie Ferrell, Jesse William Olson, Amy Quan Barry, Steve the TA at UW-Madison, Mrs Berg, Adam Gregory Pergament, Tate McClane, Leah Maines, Christen Kincaid, Jennifer Winebrenner, Kevin Maines, Jackie, and Mimi at Finishing Line Press, Alex Chappell, words, music, time, patience, and clouds that look kind of like animals and/or things.

"A Quiet Moment" and "Routine" first appeared in *The 2017 Richmond Anthology of Poetry*.

"A Quiet Moment" also appeared in *Ginosko Literary Journal*, along with "Hakomi Walk" and "What I Mean When I Say the Words."

"The Novelty of Theft," "'Essential' Work," and "Status Report" first appeared on poetryandcovid.com.

"Motorcycle," "Food of Love," "Bath Hair," and "Renewables" first appeared at the Bay Area Generations reading series.

"The Zen of Surviving" first appeared on onesentencepoems.com.

ABOUT THE AUTHOR

Born and raised in Wanamingo, MN, **David Brehmer** drifted his way to Richmond, CA in 2005, where he lives with his wife, son, dog, and drums. His work has appeared in *The MacGuffin, Humana Obscura, Ginsosko Literary Journal*, and on beatnikcowboy.com. In 2012 he co-self-published with artist Jeannine Chappell, *This Has Happened: Words and Images After the Crash*, which detailed their separate but parallel responses to the drunk driving crash that killed friend and bandmate Alex Chappell, Jeannine's son, and left David in the hospital for a month.

Life, Death, Love, and Babies is filled with thoughts and events significant and otherwise that occurred during the ten or so years since the crash.

Thank you for reading. Drive safe.

twitter.com/daviddrum22
david-brehmer.squarespace.com

www.ingramcontent.com/pod-product-compliance
Lightning Source LLC
Chambersburg PA
CBHW031124160426

43192CB00008B/1108